Paul Robeson

By JoAnn Grote

Wright Group

The McGraw·Hill Companies

www.WrightGroup.com

Wright Group

Send all inquiries to:
Wright Group/McGraw-Hill
P.O. Box 812960
Chicago, IL 60681

ISBN 1-4045-3301-X
ISBN 1-4045-3271-4 (6-pack)

1 2 3 4 5 6 7 8 9 BSF 11 10 09 08 07 06 05

Contents

Historical Time Line

Wonderful inventions and advancements in civil rights changed the world dramatically during Paul Robeson's lifetime. Moving pictures became popular, television brought events into people's homes, and radios and two-sided discs made music available to most Americans. When Paul was born, the Wright brothers hadn't yet invented the airplane. Before Paul died, man had landed on the moon. More important, minorities gained major advances in voting rights, and in educational and job opportunities.

The Spanish-American War is fought.

The Boy Scouts are founded.

The first recording is made.

On April 9, Paul Robeson is born in Princeton, New Jersey.

Paul Robeson first visits the Soviet Union.

1898   **1907**   **1918**   **1930**   **1939**

1903   **1914**   **1925**   **1934**

Paul Robeson plays Othello in London.

The Great Train Robbery, the first Western, is made.

World War I begins.

World War I ends.

The first helicopter flies.

World War II begins.

Color television is introduced in the United States.

The Civil Rights Act of 1964 is passed into law.

World War II ends.

On January 23, Paul Robeson dies.

1945

1953

1964

1976

1943

1949

1956

1969

On October 19, *Othello* opens on Broadway.

Paul Robeson speaks at the World Peace Conference in Paris.

Paul Robeson is called before House Committee on Un-American Activities.

Richard James conceived the idea of the *Slinky* toy for children.

The first human sets foot on the moon.

Author's Note

   Paul Robeson was born the year the Spanish-American war began. Like a war, much of his life was a life of conflict. He fought to prove himself as an African American in a country where many considered African Americans to be less intelligent than white people. Later, he fought for equality, respect, and dignity for oppressed people the world over.

   Paul fought battles with words and songs. He fought battles by being one of the best in the world at what he did—playing sports, acting, and singing. People all over the world saw his courage and it gave them the strength to fight for their own rights.

   I admire Paul Robeson because he stood up for what he believed no matter what the cost. Discover what Paul said and did that made people think he was special. As you read, decide whether you think this man is a truly amazing American.

JoAnn Grote

CHAPTER ONE

World-Famous Actor

*P*aul Robeson stood in his dressing room, waiting for the play to begin. The play was *Othello*, written by William Shakespeare, and Paul had the title role. Many actors and directors believed Othello was the most difficult role an actor could play. Was he ready for it?

He'd played the role in London 15 years ago to rave reviews. But deep inside, Paul had always known he hadn't yet given Othello his best. Tonight he would play Othello in his own country, the United States, on one of the world's most celebrated stages. Would his performance finally meet his own high standards?

Paul Robeson in the London performance of Othello

Paul knew he was fortunate to have the role. Many people in America thought African American actors could only play simple parts. Many roles for African American actors made them look foolish and ignorant. Paul felt it was his responsibility to prove that African Americans deserved to play dignified parts.

Robeson as Othello

Paul tried to concentrate on the performance ahead of him, but his mind wandered. Even if the audience and critics liked his acting, would they accept a black man in the role of Othello? Othello was in love with a white woman, and in most parts of the United States, a black man falling in love with a white woman was unthinkable.

It was time to go on stage. No more time to worry. Paul would give this performance the best that was in him. He could do no more than that.

Paul Robeson (right) and Jose Ferrer in Othello, *1943*

When the play was over, the audience roared! The people screamed Paul's name. That night, October 19, 1943, Paul and the other actors were called to the stage ten times to accept the audience's praise. Cheers and applause split the air for 20 minutes.

Paul Robeson and Uta Hagen in a scene from the play Othello, *1943*

Critics wrote that Paul made "a great Othello," and that he gave "a tremendous performance." One critic wrote that the play was "one of the most memorable events in the history of the theater . . . . It is unbelievably magnificent." All of Paul's hard work had paid off.

In Their Own Words

"You have rendered the Negro race and the world a great service in *Othello* by demonstrating that Negroes are capable of great and enduring interpretations in the realm of the theatre."

~Dr. Benjamin Mays, President of Morehouse College, while presenting Paul with the honorary degree of Doctor of Humane Letters in 1943

Leap Back in Time

The film industry was continuously advancing when Paul Robeson began his singing and acting career. Paul saw arts and culture in America progress from live performances and silent motion pictures to movies with audio and special effects. Radios became available for home use and often brought families and friends together to listen to news. Take a look at the pictures on these two pages. How do you think what you did for entertainment would be different if you were alive during the first half of the twentieth century?

RADIO

MOVIE
THEATER

SCIENCE'S
MONSTER
TERROR!

BORIS
KARLOFF

FRANKENSTEIN

MOVIE
POSTERS

MOVIE
CAMERA

ɔ⊃ 11

CHAPTER TWO

Paul's Early Life

On April 9, 1898, Paul Robeson was born in Princeton, New Jersey to William and Maria Louisa Robeson. He grew up in a large family, the youngest of five children. Paul's mother was a teacher from a prominent **abolitionist** family in Philadelphia. She was part African, part Native American.

Paul's father, whom Paul called "Pop," was born a slave. He escaped when he was a teenager and eventually went to college. He'd been a pastor for almost 20 years when Paul was born. But when Paul was a toddler, Pop lost his job. He barely made enough money to meet the family's needs, but he carried himself with dignity and pride.

Paul Robeson was born at this location in Princeton, New Jersey.

Paul Robeson's mother, Maria Louisa Robeson

When Paul was six, his mother died in a kitchen fire. By the time he was nine, only he and his brother, Ben, were still living with their father. Ben went to prep school and Paul moved with his father to the nearby town of Westfield. Pop worked in a grocery store and he and Paul slept in the store attic. There was a lean-to attached to the back of the store where they cooked and bathed.

When he was 12, Paul and his father moved to Somerville, New Jersey, where Pop became pastor again. **Spirituals** and the music of the church became a big part of Paul's life. "I heard my people singing!" he remembered later. "My soul was filled with their harmonies."

Paul Robeson was very close to his father, William Drew Robeson.

In Their Own Words

"The glory of my boyhood years was my father. I loved him like no one in all the world."

~*Paul Robeson on the importance of his father*

It was his brother, Bill, who discovered that Paul could sing. One hot July day, while they were just singing for fun, Bill exclaimed, "Paul, you can sing!" Paul thought Bill was teasing. But when Paul sang again, Bill again said, "Paul, you *can* sing!" For the first time, Paul realized that his voice was special.

Microphone

Pop helped Paul develop his voice for public speaking. He gave Paul speeches to memorize and taught Paul how to use his voice to make the speeches more powerful. In school, Paul's music teacher helped him develop his rich, baritone singing voice. She made him a soloist in the chorus.

Singing was one of Paul Robeson's many talents.

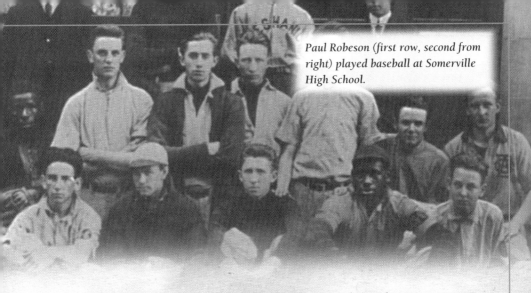

Paul Robeson (first row, second from right) played baseball at Somerville High School.

Paul attended Somerville High School where he was one of only a few African American students. He had no problems getting along with his white classmates or teachers. He thrived as a student, studying Greek, Latin, chemistry, and physics. He also excelled at singing, debating, and athletics. The school principal, however, could not stand him. The more Paul succeeded, the angrier the principal got. When Paul made a mistake, however, the principal tried to make him feel awful about it. "His sharp words were meant to make me feel as miserably inferior as he thought a Negro was," Paul later remembered.

Did You Know...

Paul Robeson was first introduced to William Shakespeare and *Othello* at Somerville High School. He was selected to play the part of Othello in the school production. When it came time to perform, Paul struggled through his lines, nervous about winning the approval of his teacher and his father. The experience was so difficult, he never imagined he would act again.

In 1915, Paul won a four-year scholarship to Rutgers College in New Jersey. He was only the third African American student to attend the school, and was the first African American athlete ever on a Rutgers team.

On the first day of practice, his football teammates ganged up on him, giving Paul a broken nose (an injury which affected his singing for the rest of his life), a sprained arm, and numerous other wounds. He spent ten days in bed recovering. Paul's teammates finally accepted him, and he helped win many

Paul Robeson played football at Rutgers College.

games. In fact, Paul excelled at several sports, becoming the first Rutgers athlete to win 12 letters—four in football, three in baseball, three in basketball, and two in track.

In Their Own Words

"I was the representative of a lot of Negro boys ... and, as their representative, I had to show I could take whatever was handed out."

~Paul Robeson on playing football and attending college

Columbia University, where Paul Robeson attended law school

Eslanda Robeson, 1950

Paul graduated from Rutgers at the top of his class and went on to attend Columbia Law School. To pay for school, he played professional football, earning up to $500 a game—a lot of money at the time.

While at Columbia, Paul met and married Eslanda Goode, a brilliant scientist. After graduating from Columbia, Paul worked as a lawyer in New York. When a white secretary refused to work for him because he was African American, Paul decided to end his law career. He wasn't sure what to do next.

CHAPTER THREE

Paul Becomes Famous

While Paul was still at Columbia, he did some acting and singing on the side. Now that he ended his law practice he would turn this side job into a career. In 1923, Paul was offered major roles in two plays by the famous writer, Eugene O'Neill: *The Emperor Jones* and *All God's Chillun Got Wings*.

In *All God's Chillun Got Wings*, Paul played a black man married to a white woman. At one point in the play, the woman kissed Paul's hand. Interracial romance was unacceptable at the time. Newspapers warned of riots if the play opened. The **Ku Klux Klan** even threatened Paul's life. But, on opening night, there was no trouble and the cast performed to thunderous applause and rave reviews.

Paul Robeson and Ruby Elzy in Emperor Jones

The next year, Paul made his first movie, a silent film called *Body and Soul*. A year later, he gave a concert of Negro spirituals, and put out his first recording. Paul's life was moving at whirlwind speed. Before the record was released, he was in London, England starring in a play called *The Emperor Jones*.

Paul Robeson and Mary Blair in
All God's Chillun Got Wings

In 1928, while still in London, Paul played one of his most famous roles in the musical play, *Show Boat*. He played Joe, a poor Mississippi River ship worker. Paul's performance of *"Ol' Man River,"* a song about the hardships of Joe's life, was so moving that it became associated with Paul for the rest of his life.

Robeson's "Ol' Man River"

Paul Robeson changed the original "Ol' Man River" lyrics to reflect the African American struggle for equality.

Original by Jerome Kern:	Robeson's rewrite:
Ah gits weary	*But I keeps laughing*
An' sick of tryin',	*Instead of crying,*
Ah'm tired of livin'	*I must keep fighting*
An' skeered of dyin',	*Until I'm dying,*
But Ol' Man River,	*And Ol' Man River,*
He jes' keeps rollin' along	*He just keeps rolling along!*

Chinese calligraphy by Paul Robeson, 1950s

While living in England, Paul came to realize that common, working people were the heart and soul of a nation, not the wealthy people who often came to see his concerts. He began to learn the music of the working class—folksongs and work songs. They reminded him of the spirituals he loved and he felt the music could be a bridge between cultures.

Paul learned several languages so he could sing the folk and work songs as they were originally written. Eventually, he could speak 27 languages. Paul was inspired to work not only for the rights of African Americans, but for the rights of **oppressed** people all over the world.

Paul Robeson in picket line protesting racial segregation in theater, Baltimore, Maryland, 1947

In Their Own Words

". . . the common people of all nations are truly brothers in the great family of mankind."

~Paul Robeson

Among the languages Paul learned were several African dialects. He and Eslanda had met many Africans in London, and Paul began to see himself as African, too.

One of Paul's African friends told him about the Yakut people in the Soviet Union. The Yakuts were once mistreated in much the same way some American white people

Paul often spoke for the rights of oppressed people.

mistreated black people. When the Soviet Union became a **communist** state, the Yakuts finally got the equal treatment they deserved. Paul was fascinated, and in 1934 he went to the Soviet Union to see for himself how the Yakuts lived.

Paul Robeson and wife, Eslanda, arrive in the U.S. after a successful European tour, 1935

In the Soviet Union, Paul was treated with a level of respect he did not always enjoy as an African American man in the United States. What impressed him most was that all Soviet school children were educated against **racism**. He wanted his son, nine-year-old Paul Jr., to grow up in such an environment, so he placed Paul Jr. in a Soviet school.

Paul Robeson (left) taught his son, Paul Jr. (right), to respect people regardless of race.

Paul believed it was time the United States followed the Soviet Union's example.

In Their Own Words

"Here, for the first time in my life . . . I walk in full human dignity."

~*Paul Robeson on the Soviet Union*

CHAPTER FOUR

Hard Years for Paul and America

*I*n the late 1940s and early 1950s, the United States was extremely suspicious of the Soviet Union. Communism was very different from the American system of government. These differences caused each nation to see the other as an enemy. If the two nations went to war, the United States government feared that Americans who supported communism might help the Soviets win. The government forced suspected communists and communist supporters to defend themselves before a group called the House Un-American Activities Committee. If someone was called before the committee, there was a good chance his or her career would be ruined.

Joseph Stalin was the head of the Soviet Union from 1929–1953.

Paul Robeson spoke at the World Peace Conference in Paris on April 20, 1949.

In the 1940s, Paul's career was at its height. He gave several speeches challenging racism in America and expressing support for the Soviet system of equality. The **FBI** began to watch him. By the late 1940s, according to Paul Robeson Jr., the FBI pressured American concert halls to cancel Paul's concerts.

America's fear of war with the Soviet Union was also at its height. In 1949, Paul gave a speech at a peace conference in Paris, France. According to American newspapers, Paul said that if a war with the Soviets occurred, African Americans should not be expected to fight. The papers quoted Paul as saying:

> It is unthinkable that American Negroes would go to war on behalf of those who have oppressed us for generations against a country (the Soviet Union) which in one generation has raised our people to the full dignity of mankind.

The American people were outraged. Before long, Paul was accused of being a communist and called to defend himself before the House Un-American Activities Committee.

Police hold back protestors at a rally near Robeson's concert in Peekskill, New York.

The next year, the government took away Paul's **passport** so he could not leave the United States. He could have his passport back if he signed a statement agreeing not to make any more speeches. Paul refused to sign. He continued to speak out against racism in a newspaper he started called *Freedom*.

This effigy was hung to protest Robeson's 1949 performance in Peekskill, New York.

For nearly a decade, Paul was **blacklisted** from concert halls, movie studios, and theaters. His income, which had been over $100,000 in 1947, dropped to about $2,000 in 1950. He also lost a number of friends and supporters, including several **civil rights** groups. His trophies were no longer displayed at Rutgers University, and he was banned from the College Football Hall of Fame.

Did You Know...

According to Paul Robeson Jr., his father never said African Americans shouldn't fight in a war against the Soviet Union. He claims that the quote that ran in the newspapers was a combination of bits and pieces from other speeches Robeson gave.

Those who still believed in Paul found ways around the U.S. government's restrictions. In 1952, a group from Canada arranged for Paul to perform at Peace Arch Park on the Canadian-U.S. border. "I shall always remember that concert on May 18, 1952, when 30,000 Canadians came from miles away to hear me," Paul wrote later. Groups from Europe later found ways for Paul to perform over the phone. One such concert in England was organized by members of the British government.

Robeson talks with Nikita Khrushchev, Soviet Union leader, 1959

Joseph Stalin

Under communism, the people of the Soviet Union did not enjoy the freedoms Americans enjoyed. Soviets who spoke out against the government were often imprisoned or executed. This is partly why Americans were so opposed to communism. However, when the U.S. government went after American communist supporters, many Americans were stripped of their rights and privileges.

Paul Robeson spoke before the House Un-American Activities Committee, Washington, D.C., June 13, 1956.

Paul's trial before the Un-American Activities Committee came in 1956. He didn't deny his respect for the Soviet Union, but he did not say he was a communist. When he was asked why he didn't move to the Soviet Union, Paul replied, "Because my father was a slave, and my people died to build this country, and I am going to stay here and have a part of it just like you."

Did You Know... Paul's great-great-grandfather, Cyrus Bustill, was a slave who bought his own freedom. He baked bread for George Washington's troops during the Revolutionary War.

Two years later, Paul won his passport battle and could travel again. Before going abroad for a concert tour which included London, Berlin, and Russia, he gave a sold-out concert at Carnegie Hall, one of the finest theaters in the United States. That same year, Paul published his autobiography, *Here I Stand*.

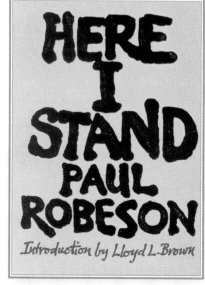

Paul Robeson wrote his autobiography, Here I Stand, *in 1958.*

In 1963, after a successful tour abroad, Paul returned to the United States. His health was poor, and he had been hospitalized many times on his trip. Still, he remained active and began to regain a bit of the American support he had once enjoyed. A concert in his honor was held

in 1965. It was organized and attended by a number of prominent African American writers and entertainers.

Paul Robeson meets with reporters after returning from Europe.

That same year, his wife Eslanda died of cancer. Except for a few appearances, Paul withdrew from public life and moved to Philadelphia, Pennsylvania to live with his sister, Marian. He lived there until his death in 1976.

When he grew older, Paul Robeson lived until the end of his life with his sister, Marian.

Honoring Paul Robeson

Throughout his life, Paul received many honors and awards. Here are just a few:

Two-Time All-American Football Player, 1917–1918

Abraham Lincoln Medal for Notable and Distinguished Service in Human Relations in New York, 1943

Medal for Good Diction on the State from American Academy of Arts and Letters, 1944

Donaldson Award for Outstanding Lead Performance (Othello), 1944

National Association for the Advancement of Colored People's Spingarn Medal for highest achievement by a black American, 1945

National Church of Nigeria names Paul "Champion of African Freedom," 1950

Stalin Peace Prize, 1953

Paul Robeson established a choir in Berlin, German Democratic Republic, that became the Paul Robeson Choir in 1964

Conclusion

Paul Robeson is featured on a 2004 United States postage stamp.

Paul Robeson wanted his country to be the country its constitution and Bill of Rights said it was: a land of equal opportunities, where citizens could believe what they wished and say what they believed. His courage inspired others to speak out in spite of the risks.

As an African American born in the United States during a time when African Americans were routinely denied equal opportunities in education and jobs, it was Paul who exceeded the career expectations of most men, black or white. However, he did more than use his talents to make money for himself. Paul Robeson dedicated his life to uplifting African Americans and others who did not enjoy the liberties they deserved.

Paul Robeson Jr. speaks at the dedication of the stamp honoring his father on January 20, 2004.

Glossary

abolitionist a person who worked to end slavery

blacklisted a person's name being publicly listed for disapproval or punishment

civil rights the rights enjoyed by a citizen of a country, including the freedom from discrimination

communist a person or group that believes a single group of people should have complete control over a country's goods and services

FBI (Federal Bureau of Investigation) an investigative unit of the U.S. government

Ku Klux Klan a secret organization whose members believe white people are superior to all others

oppressed mistreated by people with more power

passport a document allowing a person to travel between countries

racism the belief that one race is superior to another

spirituals religious songs developed among African Americans in the United States

Index